LET'S ROCK!

What Are Sedimentary Rocks?

Natalie Hyde

Crabtree Publishing Company
www.crabtreebooks.com

Author: Natalie Hyde
Editor-in-Chief: Paul Challen
Project coordinator: Kathy Middleton
Proofreaders: Rachel Stuckey, Crystal Sikkens
Photo research: Melissa McClellan
Designer: Tibor Choleva
Production coordinator: Amy Salter
Production: Kim Richardson
Prepress technician: Amy Salter

Consultant: Kelsey McCormack, B.Sc, M.Sc, PhD
McMaster University

Title page: Rock found in Quebrada de Humauaca, Argentina

Special Thanks: Stu Harding, Lucyna Bethune,
Sandor Monos and Sandee Ewasiuk

This book was produced for Crabtree Publishing Company
by Silver Dot Publishing.

Illustrations:
© David Brock: pages 19, 24

Photographs and reproductions:
© Dreamstime.com: pages 14 (Zirafek), 15 middle (Photawa), 15 bottom small (Yukosourov)

© istockphoto.com: pages 4(wolv), 5 middle (Petegar), 7 bottom (PMUDU), 11 bottom (MarkoHeuver), 11 top (Noosa Aerial), 14 top (sxcurry), 16 (mariusFM77), 16/17 large (iropa), 22 bottom (Zandebasenjis), 23 right bottom (pomarinus)

© Shutterstock.com: headline image (CLM), background image (CLM), title page (thoron), pages 4/5 large (akva), 5 top (markrhiggins), 6/7 large (Hung Chung Chih), 6 (Denys Poliakov), 7 top (B.G. Smith), 8/9 large (Katrina Leigh), 9 top (akva), 10 bottom (Laurin Rinder), 10 top (AridOcean), 11 middle (iBird), 12 (thoron), 13 top (Tom Grundy), 13 bottom (SF photo),15 bottom (Xin Qiu), 17 top (Yury Kosourov), 17 middle left (Brian Brockman),17 middle right (Carolina K. Smith, M.D.), 18 top (Standa Riha), 18/19 large (ailenn), 19 top (douglas knight), 19 bottom (Alexey Stiop), 20 middle (Denis and Yulia Pogostins), 20/21 large (vitek12), 21 top (Manamana), 21 bottom (Jarrod Boord), 22/23 large (Neale Cousland), 23 top (Gary Andrews), 23 right top (Kletr), 23 right middle (kkymek), 24/25 large (IPK Photography), 25 top (Falk Kienas), 26/27 large (Kenneth Keifer), 27 bottom (Sharon Day), 28 top (Jeffrey Liao), 28 bottom (sculpies), 28 bottom left (mmmm), 29 top (Brandon Jennings), 29 middle (Elena Elisseeva), 29 bottom (dcb)

© Spectrum Photofile Inc., photographersdirect.com: page 15 top

© Werner Forman Archive, photographersdirect.com: page 22 top

© AR Studio Inc., photographersdirect.com: page 25 middle

© Fotosearch: page 27 middle

© NASA: page 9 middle

Public Domain pages 16 lower left (Wilson44691), 22 bottom left (Beruthiel)

Library and Archives Canada Cataloguing in Publication

Hyde, Natalie, 1963-
What are sedimentary rocks? / Natalie Hyde.

(Let's rock)
Includes index.
Issued also in an electronic format.
ISBN 978-0-7787-7230-9 (bound).--ISBN 978-0-7787-7235-4 (pbk.)

1. Rocks, Sedimentary--Juvenile literature. I. Title. II. Series:
Let's rock (St. Catharines, Ont.)

QE471.H93 2011   j552'.5   C2010-904132-1

Library of Congress Cataloging-in-Publication Data

Hyde, Natalie, 1963-
What are sedimentary rocks? / Natalie Hyde.
p. cm. -- (Let's rock)
Includes index.
ISBN 978-0-7787-7230-9 (reinforced lib. bdg. : alk. paper) -- ISBN 978-0-7787-7235-4 (pbk. : alk. paper) -- ISBN 978-1-4271-9524-1 (electronic (pdf))
1. Rocks, Sedimentary--Juvenile literature. 2. Petrology--Juvenile literature.
I. Title. II. Series.

QE471.H93 2011
552'.5--dc22
                                2010024600

Crabtree Publishing Company
www.crabtreebooks.com   1-800-387-7650

Printed in the U.S.A./082010/BA20100709

Published in Canada
Crabtree Publishing
616 Welland Ave.
St. Catharines, Ontario
L2M 5V6

Published in the United States
Crabtree Publishing
PMB 59051
350 Fifth Avenue, 59th Floor
New York, New York 10118

Published in the United Kingdom
Crabtree Publishing
Maritime House
Basin Road North, Hove
BN41 1WR

Published in Australia
Crabtree Publishing
386 Mt. Alexander Rd.
Ascot Vale (Melbourne)
VIC 3032

CONTENTS

WHERE DID IT ALL BEGIN?

Out of the three types of rock, **igneous**, sedimentary, and **metamorphic**, sedimentary is the most common. It is made up of layers of small particles that are pressed and cemented tightly together.

CLASTIC ROCKS

Different kinds of particles make different kinds of sedimentary rocks. Sandstone and shale are made up of bits of other rocks and minerals and are called **clastic** rocks.

ORGANIC ROCKS

Other sedimentary rocks, such as coal or chalk, are mostly formed by the remains of plants or animals. Because they are made up mostly of things that were once alive, they are called organic sedimentary rocks.

▶ *Coal is the largest source of energy for the generation of electricity.*

▶ *Nearly 40 major sedimentary rock layers are exposed in the Grand Canyon.*

WEAK OR STRONG?

✳ Some sedimentary rocks, such as shale, are so soft you can crumble them in your hand. Others, such as quartz sandstone, are so hard you can barely break them apart with a sledgehammer.

▼ *Shale is a rather soft sedimentary rock.*

BRING OUT YOUR DEAD!

Fossils are found in sedimentary rock. They are the ancient remains of plants and animals.

▶ *Well-preserved fossil of a prehistoric fish*

◀ *Limestone rock is made up mostly of calcite.*

CHEMICAL ROCKS

Minerals or chemicals form the third type of sedimentary rocks. For example, limestone is made up mostly of a mineral called **calcite**. It is known as a chemical sedimentary rock.

MAKE YOUR OWN ROCK

(Have an adult help you with this activity.)

You will need:

- mixing bowl
- small paper cup
- Epsom salts
- spoon
- sand
- water

Mix 1 cup of water and ½ cup of Epsom salts in a mixing bowl. Stir until most of the salts have dissolved. Fill a paper cup halfway with sand. Now add just enough salt solution to wet the sand. Let dry for two or three days. Cut away the paper cup.

Where did the salt go? How did it help form the rock?

WEARING IT AWAY

Ice, wind, rain, flowing rivers, glaciers, waves, and natural chemicals all wear away at human-made and natural structures on Earth. The particles that fall off these structures create the sediment that can form into sedimentary rock.

WEATHERING

Weathering is the breaking down of Earth's soil, rocks, and minerals by weather, chemical reactions, and plants and animals. The movement of rocks, minerals, and soil by forces such as water, ice, wind, and **gravity** is called **erosion**.

HEAVY METAL

✳ The same chemicals that can eat away at rocks also break down metals. One common form of **corrosion** is rust, which you can see on cars, garbage cans, and other metal objects all around you.

▼ *Rust is a common form of corrosion.*

▶ *Mountain river transporting large amounts of sediment*

WHO DOO?

Hoodoos are sandstone structures created by weathering. The **capstone** on top is made of harder rock than the columns. It protects the softer rock underneath, creating formations called rock mushrooms.

▼ *Hoodoos found in the badlands of Alberta, Canada*

CORROSION

Chemicals in the air, whether from pollution or volcanic eruptions, can make rainwater **acidic**. This solution will eat away at many surfaces, including rocks.

TRANSPORTATION

When parts of a rock break off and wear away, they are carried off by moving ice, water, or wind. This part of erosion is called transportation. The material carried away by rivers is called the **load**. Some rivers turn brown or yellow when they are carrying large amounts of sediment.

DEPOSITION

Glaciers carry sediment down mountains and eventually deposit them in one spot. When rivers reach an ocean or a lake they slow down and also deposit the eroded sediment. In deserts, wind carries small sand particles long distances, piling the sand into large dunes. In all these cases, this build-up is called deposition. Where these deposits build up, sedimentary rock can form.

▼ *Acid rain can produce cracks in limestone slabs called clints.*

ICE, WIND, AND WATER

Erosion is nature's way of using elements over and over again. Bits of rock, minerals, plants, and animals are moved and used to create something new.

WIND EROSION

Wind erosion has the power to scrape and polish solid rock with small sand particles that act like sandpaper. Pushing one grain at a time, wind can cause sand dunes to move several feet each year.

▼ *Arches and towers created by wind erosion*

WASHED AWAY

You will need:
- sand
- sand shovel
- buckets
- water

Build a sandcastle.

Fill a bucket with water.

Pour a little water slowly over part of the sandcastle. Watch what happens.

Now pour a lot of water very quickly over the sandcastle. Watch what happens.

Why do you think there is a difference?

MOVE IT!

To create the Grand Canyon, the Colorado River moved about 30,000 dump truck loads of sediment every day.

▶ *The Colorado River started carving the Grand Canyon at least 17 million years ago.*

WATER EROSION

Running water is one of the most powerful forces on Earth. It breaks down and transports tons of material. That is why most sedimentary rock is formed underwater in riverbeds or at the bottom of the ocean. The most sediment is moved during floods because more water than normal is moving at a much faster rate.

GLACIAL EROSION

Glaciers form and move very slowly, but they have carved out and moved huge amounts of earth and rocks over time. They create sediment with their weight and size by pushing and scraping out valleys. The sediment is deposited along the glacier's path and in the lakes created when the ice melts.

▼ *Satelite view of Bodélé Depression*

BLOWN AWAY

✳ Scientists have used satellites to determine that the sand dunes in the Bodélé Depression, in Chad, are some of the fastest moving on Earth.

9

MAKING A DEPOSIT

Eventually gravity will force wind, water, and ice to drop their load. The places where the sediment collects in deep layers are the beginning of new sedimentary rock.

GETTING IN THE WAY

Wind can carry small particles high in the air for long distances. As the air current slows, gravity pulls the fine silt or sand down to the ground. If the wind is stopped suddenly by a large object such as a cliff, building, or fence, the particles will pile up in front of it.

▼ *Some dunes can rise up to 650 feet (198 m) high.*

DROP ZONE

✳ The Nile River delta is one of the largest in the world. In some places the topsoil is 70 feet (21 m) deep.

▼ *Aerial view of the Nile River delta*

FLOODPLAIN AND DELTA

Rivers can push larger material along the river bottom, while smaller particles are **suspended** or even **dissolved** in the water and can travel long distances. If a river bends, the current slows on the outer edge and sediment builds up. Other particles continue on until the river meets a larger body of water, such as a lake or ocean, and stops flowing. This causes sediment to build up where the two meet creating sandbars. This area is called a delta.

MELTING INTO MORAINES

Glaciers carry clay, sand, rocks, and boulders, which are deposited at the sides and front of the glacier. These mounds of debris are called moraines.

▲ Sandbars at the Noosa River delta

▲ **Floodplains** form alongside shallow rivers. When a river overflows, sediment leaves the river and remains confined to the floodplain.

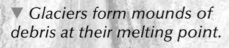

▼ Glaciers form mounds of debris at their melting point.

THE LAYERED LOOK

As different forces of erosion move particles around and deposit them, the sediment builds up in layers. These layers, called strata or beds, give us a record of the environment at a moment in time. Some strata are thin, while others are several meters thick.

▼ *Layers of sediments can be very colorful.*

SETTLE DOWN!

See how sediment at the bottom of rivers arranges itself in layers.

You will need:
- a glass jar with lid
- soil
- fine gravel
- small rocks
- sand
- water

Put the soil, sand, gravel, and rocks into the jar (no more than half full). Fill with water. Put on lid and shake until well mixed. Set the jar down and let the ingredients settle.

How did the different materials arrange themselves?

THE LAKE EFFECT

A flash flood might deposit a lot of silt and clay on a floodplain. Later, a thin layer of ash from a volcanic eruption might cover the area. Hundreds of years later, a glacier might deposit crushed rock. When the glacier melts, it might leave behind a lake where small marine animals shed their shells. Each event would leave its own unique layer of material.

BEDDING DOWN

Thousands of years later, these strata would form a sedimentary rock with different colors and textures. Between the strata are horizontal surfaces called bedding planes. Sedimentary rocks tend to separate or break along these planes.

▲ Slanted layers are formed by fast moving water or wind.

◄ Tews Falls in Dundas, Ontario, Canada

LAYERS OF TIME

The Niagara Escarpment is a ridge of sedimentary rock hundreds of miles long that stretches from Niagara Falls to Tobermory in Ontario, Canada. The strata are full of rocks and fossils as old as 500 million years.

A CLAST ACT

Most sedimentary rocks are clastic. This means they are made from mud, sand, or pieces of other rocks called **clasts**. Most fossils are found in this type of sedimentary rock.

▼ *A large boulder of conglomerate rock*

CONGLOMERATES

Some of the clasts can be the size of marbles and are cemented together by minerals in the water. These rocks are called conglomerates when the clasts are worn smooth from erosion. They are called breccia when they still have sharp edges. They are often found where there has been landslides or in glacial moraines. These are places where particles of all different sizes were deposited together.

▼ *Conglomerate rock called Pudding Stone*

FOSSIL FRENZY

A large shale deposit in the Burgess Pass in British Columbia, Canada, is famous for the number and quality of fossils found there. The creatures probably became trapped in mud that flowed over a 328-foot (100 m) cliff and collected at the bottom turning into shale centuries later.

◄ *Visitors in the Burgess Pass examining fossils in the shale*

A LITTLE FLAKEY

Mud is made of particles of rock crushed as fine as flour. When mud is the main sediment, shale or mudstone is created. The bedding planes in shale are very thin, causing it to flake off easily.

SANDY AND HANDY

Sandstone can be different colors depending on what other minerals are layered with the sand. A lot of **feldspar** in sandstone creates a tan color, while iron will produce a reddish sandstone. If the sand particles are cemented together with quartz, the sandstone will be very strong. If it is held together with clay, it may be soft enough to rub off in your hands.

▲ *Mudstone formations in the badlands of Alberta, Canada, are full of fossils.*

▼ *Feldspar minerals are found in many types of sedimentary rock.*

CHEMISTRY IN ACTION

Some sedimentary rocks are formed by material that dissolves in water. Salt, calcite, and silica are all minerals that form chemical sedimentary rocks.

ALL DRIED UP

Rock salt is a sedimentary rock that forms when saltwater lakes or seas **evaporate**. Some rock salt deposits are deep underground and were formed thousands of years ago when the area was underwater.

▶ *Salt formations at the Dead Sea in the Middle East*

HIGH AND DRY

How does rock salt form?

You will need:
- large glass bowl
- measuring cup
- tablespoon
- table salt

Pour 1 cup of water into the glass bowl. Add 4 tablespoons of salt and stir until all the salt is dissolved. Allow the bowl to sit undisturbed until all the water has evaporated. (This might take three to four weeks.)

Are some crystals different from others? Why?

▼ *Rock salt creates crystals.*

GO LONG!

✳ Some Native Americans used flint to make spear tips and stone tools. To make an arrowhead or spear point, the piece of flint is hit with a rock. The sides flake off to produce a sharp edge.

OH–OH...IT'S OOLITE!

Sometimes, minerals such as calcite form around a small grain of quartz or a tiny piece of shell. This small, coated grain is called an ooid. Pressed tightly together, these ooids look like fish eggs. Oolite is sedimentary rock formed from ooids and is part of the limestone family.

▼ Ooids look like fish eggs.

SILLY SILICA

Some kinds of sedimentary rocks are made from a chemical called silica. Flint and chert are two kinds of this type of rock.

▲ Chert can be easily broken into sharp flakes.

LIME IS FINE

Limestone is a sedimentary rock mainly composed of the mineral calcite. The source of calcite is usually marine **organisms** deposited on the ocean floors.

Magnesium is a mineral common in seawater. Magnesium-rich deposits form dolomitic limestone.

▼ The Dolomites in Northern Italy are a section of the Alps.

GOING UNDERGROUND

The earth under our feet is not always solid rock. Underground water eats away at the sedimentary rock and creates holes, caves, and caverns. Caves are a natural shelter and have been used not only by animals, but by humans, too.

LIMESTONE BEAUTY

The **calcium carbonate** in limestone is easily dissolved by water. An area that has a lot of limestone soon becomes full of caves and channels and is called a karst landscape.

▼ *Krka River in Slovenia flows through one of the most beautiful karst landscapes.*

GO LONG!

✳ The longest cave system in the world is in Mammoth Cave National Park in Kentucky. It is so long, in fact, that if you combine the second and third longest cave systems, the Mammoth Caves are still longer by 100 miles (160 km)!

▼ *A typical limestone cave entrance*

WHAT A DRIP!

Water that seeps into caves often contains minerals. It might drip slowly in through cracks in the ceiling or walls. As the water evaporates, it leaves behind the minerals that form rock structures. Icicle-shaped stalactites hang down from the ceiling. When the water drips to the floor, stalagmite towers form.

◀ *When stalactites and stalagmites meet, they create columns.*

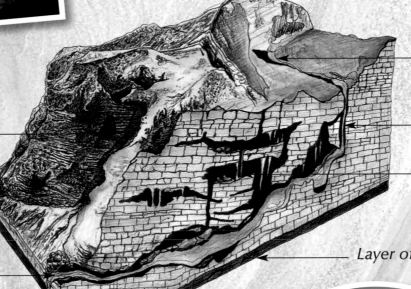

Sinkhole

Pothole and vertical shaft

Stalactites and stalagmites

Layer of nonporous rock

Cave entrance

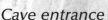

Underground stream

THAT SINKING FEELING

Sometimes, the roof of a limestone cave has been eaten away so much that the top collapses and creates a sinkhole. Sinkholes can be large enough to swallow cars and houses.

▶ *Montezuma's Well in Arizona, is a large sinkhole, 368 feet (112 m) across and 55 feet (17 m) deep.*

GOING ORGANIC

Organic material is anything that comes from plants or animals. Sediment from shells, seeds, and bones can also build up and form sedimentary rock.

SHELL GAME

Marine animals are able to use minerals dissolved in water to create their shells. Calcite is a main ingredient in seashells, and when these creatures shed their shells they fall to the seabed. Other minerals fill in the spaces between the shells and cement them all together to form **coquina**.

LITTLE LAYERS

Some of these marine animals are so tiny that their shells are the size of the head of a pin. Layers and layers of these pinhead-sized shells build up and, under pressure, form a white limestone called chalk.

▼ *Seashells contain a lot of calcite.*

POLYPS IN ACTION

Coral reefs are an important environment for many sea creatures. Coral polyps are tiny tube-shaped creatures. They form hard shells to protect their soft bodies. When the polyps die, the hard shells remain. Reefs grow larger each time new polyps attach themselves to the old tubes and form a new shell.

WHITE STUFF

✳ The White Cliffs of Dover, in England, are made of chalk, a type of limestone. The chalk we use on blackboards is actually a different mineral called gypsum.

▲ *The White Cliffs of Dover are composed mainly of chalk.*

▲ *Coral reefs are formed from the remains of living organisms.*

▼ *Stomatolite formations on Australia's coast*

SLIMY!

Ancient bacteria on the seabed helped produce a sedimentary rock called a stomatolite. The slime of the sticky bacteria would trap grains of sand and shells. This mixture would cement together with the calcium carbonate **secreted** by the bacteria.

THE COAL

Coal is an amazing organic rock. It is formed by dead and decaying plant material that is collected and pressed down over millions of years.

A SLOW PROCESS

Most plant materials, such as bark, leaves, and stems, decay quickly when exposed to air. When this material falls into the water in swamps or bogs, it is not exposed to oxygen so it decays very slowly. Peat is a brown mixture of partially decayed plant material that often forms in bogs and swamps.

BOG MUMMIES

✳ Peat bogs preserve organic material extremely well. Numerous human bodies have been found preserved in peat bogs. Some of these natural mummies are believed to be thousands of years old.

▼ *Well-preserved mummy found in a peat bog*

ON FIRE!

✳ Underground coal fires are very difficult to put out. The oldest known coal fire has been burning under Australia's Burning Mountain for more than 6,000 years!

▼ *Red ashes on Burning Mountain*

JUST CALL ME "PEAT"

Bacteria living in still water give off carbon which soaks into organic material. Over time the carbon builds up and the organic material is **compacted**. The deeper this material lies, the more pressure it is subjected to and the more carbon it contains. The more carbon found in coal, the more energy it gives off when burned. Peat can be used for fuel and contains about 60 percent carbon.

▲ *Peat is used for home fires in parts of Ireland.*

◀ *Coal was formed from ancient plants like cycads that still grow today.*

CRUMBLY STUFF

Lignite is a sedimentary rock that is created when peat has been under pressure and high temperatures deep underground. It is crumbly and often called brown coal.

▲ *Brown coal*

HIGH ENERGY

Coal is a matte, black color and comes from **compressed** lignite. It is mined in underground tunnels or open pits. Black coal produces a lot of energy when it is burned. It is the type of coal used to generate power and run industry.

▼ *Black coal*

ALMOST COMPLETELY CARBON!

If a layer of coal buckles and folds and is metamorphosed during mountain building, it becomes a harder, **denser** rock called anthracite. Anthracite is made up of almost 100 percent carbon.

▼ *Anthracite is the highest quality coal.*

FOSSILS

Fossils are traces of organisms that lived long ago. By studying fossils, scientists can learn about life-forms and their environments thousands of years ago.

RAPID BREAKDOWN

When a plant or animals dies, their parts usually break down quickly. Sometimes, the remains are buried by sediment. Without air or bacteria, the material doesn't decay. As layers of sediment build up, the material is pressed and preserved in the rock.

▶ Fossil preserved in a rock

UP FROM THE DEEP

Fossils deep in the earth are brought to the surface by Earth's forces. Mountain-building raises up Earth's crust and erosion wears away the surface.

▲ An animal is buried in the sediment on the seafloor.

▲ Other layers of sediment cover the bones.

▼ *Ants trapped in amber*

THE BIG COVER-UP

(Have an adult help you with this activity.)

You will need:

- small saucepan
- 9 x 9 inch pan lined with wax paper
- one package of chocolate chips
- small bits of candy, coconut, etc.

Melt the chocolate in the saucepan over low heat. When melted, pour a layer into the lined pan. Set pieces of candy or coconut here and there in the layer of chocolate. These are your plant and animal remains. Cover with another layer of chocolate. Repeat, adding candy or coconut. Finish with another layer of chocolate. Let cool and set.

This is how fossils become trapped in sediment and harden into rock. Have fun fossil hunting!

▶ *Fossilized skull of the Argentinian Terror Bird*

STICKY STUFF

Some plant and insect material becomes trapped in sticky tree **resin**. The resin hardens as amber and the fossils are preserved inside.

BIG BIRD

✳ The largest bird fossil ever found belongs to the 10-foot (3 m) tall Terror Bird that stalked the grasslands of ancient Argentina.

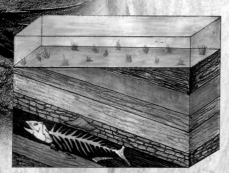

▲ *The weight of soil deposits compress the fossil's bones.*

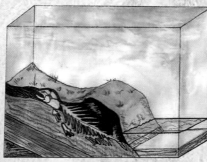

▲ *The erosion process exposes the fossil.*

READING ROCKS

Scientists are able to learn a lot about Earth through sedimentary rocks. The different layers of rock are like pages in a book. Each one tells a story about the climate, plants, and animals in the past.

IMAGINING THE PAST

Scientists know that limestone is created from the shells of sea creatures. When they see this sedimentary rock, they know the area was once underwater even if now it is in a mountain range. Sandstone might suggest an area was once a desert.

▶ *Layers of volcanic ash stand out from the other layers.*

BITE-SIZED

Some fossils and layers of sediment are helpful for identifying a certain period of time. Trilobites were little marine creatures that had a hard outer shell that made a very clear fossil. They were very widespread and evolved quickly. They are very good **index fossils**.

▲ *Trilobites are the most diverse group of extinct animals preserved in the fossil record.*

TERRIBLE LIZARD

✱ The word "dinosaur" translates to "terrible lizard." When Sir Richard Owen came up with the name in 1842, it began a worldwide interest in the creatures.

▼ *Sir Richard Owen was an English biologist and paleontologist.*

HOW OLD ARE YOU?

Fossils in sedimentary rock are an important tool in **geology**. When English engineer William Smith built canals in the early 1800s, he noticed something about the fossils in the rock. He saw that each layer of rock had very different types of fossils from those in the layers above and below. He realized that it would be possible to tell the age of rock simply by the fossils found there.

UP AND DOWN

Some layers of sediment help show a moment in history and are called **marker beds**. A layer of volcanic ash from a known eruption is a good way to date layers of rock above and below.

▼ *Marker beds can be clearly seen on the mountain formations in the Badlands National Park in South Dakota.*

THE HUMAN TOUCH

People rely on sedimentary rocks every day for everything from buildings and fuel to eyeglasses and toothpaste.

BUILDING ON THE PAST

Some of the most famous buildings in the world have been made of limestone and sandstone. The Great Pyramid in Egypt was made of millions of limestone blocks. The outer **casing stones** were a harder type of limestone than the inner stones. These white blocks were added to help protect the pyramid from weathering but most have been removed.

ROSE RED CITY

✱ Petra is a beautiful city hidden in the mountains of Jordan. The buildings were not built with blocks, but were carved into the red sandstone cliffs.

▼ *Petra was established sometime around 500 BC.*

▼ *Limestone in pyramids shows considerable signs of weathering.*

BIG BUILDING MATERIAL

Almost all stone **cathedrals**, government buildings, and castles around the world are made of limestone. It was not difficult to find and was easy to carve into blocks for more detailed designs. Notre Dame Cathedral in Paris, France; Buckingham Palace in London, England; the Empire State Building in New York, U.S.A.; and the Parliament Buildings in Ottawa, Canada, are all made of limestone.

▶ *The Empire State Building was the world's tallest building for more than 40 years.*

SOIL INGREDIENTS

The Romans used limestone, sand, gravel, and water to make concrete. They used this mixture to create some of their amazing architecture such as the Colosseum, the Pantheon, and the **aqueducts**.

▲ *Roman aqueducts were used to carry water to towns.*

NICKNAME

✳ So many buildings in Kingston, Ontario, Canada, were made of limestone, that it has been called Limestone City.

◀ *Toothpaste contains limestone powder to help clean teeth.*

SO MANY USES

Sandstone and limestone can also be ground down and heated until they melt. When the liquid cools, it forms the glass we use to make windows, dishes, and eyeglasses. Limestone is also added to toothpaste to make it rough to help clean teeth.

GLOSSARY

acidic When a liquid can eat away at other materials

aqueduct A channel, tunnel, or pipe that moves water from one place to another

calcite A mineral that helps form limestone

calcium carbonate A chemical mixture found in seashells

capstone A stone sitting on top of a stone column

casing stones A stone used as an outer covering

cathedral A large and important church

clast A fragment or piece of rock

clastic Rock made from pieces of other rocks

compacted Particles moved close together

compressed Squeezed together under pressure

coquina A rock that is mostly made of shells and shell fragments

coral reef An underwater structure made of the skeletons of sea creatures

corrosion The erosion of metals

cross bedding Tilted layers of sedimentary rock

denser Particles are packed closer together

dissolved In a liquid solution

erosion Moving solids from one place to another

evaporate To lose liquid into the air

feldspar A very hard mineral

floodplain Flat land next to a stream or river that is covered by water during a flood

geology The study of Earth through rocks

glacier A slow-moving mass of ice

gravity The force that holds things on Earth

igneous Rocks formed from magma

index fossil A type of fossil that comes from a very specific period in time

load The sediment being carried

marker beds A layer of sediment that comes from a very specific period in time

metamorphic Rock that has been changed by heat or pressure

organism A living thing

resin A thick, sticky liquid produced by trees

secrete To release or ooze a substance

suspended Kept from falling

MORE INFORMATION

FURTHER READING

Geology Rocks!: 50 Hands-On Activities to Explore the Earth.
  Cindy Blobaum. Ideals Publications Williamson Books. 2008.

Rocks and Fossils.
  Martyn Bramwell, Ian Jackson, Alan Suttie. Usborne Books. 1994.

Sedimentary Rocks.
  Melissa Stewart. Heinemann. 2002.

Rocks and Minerals.
  Britannica Illustrated Science Library. 2009.

Rocks, Minerals, and Resources series.
  Crabtree Publishing Company. 2004/2005.

WEBSITES

Geology for Kids
www.kidsgeo.com

Rocks For Kids
www.rocksforkids.com

Rocks and Minerals
http://42explore.com/rocks.htm

The Rock Identification Key
www.rockhounds.com/rockshop/rockkey/index.html

Underground Adventures
www.caverntours.com/KIDSPAGE_Formations.html

Kids Love 2Learn
www.2learn.ca/kids/science/listSciG3.asp?ID2=40

INDEX